HERE THERE IS A HOUSE STILL WORTH
ROOMS AND OF ITS SUITES, ALL BUILT
ALL THE KINGS AND ALL THE PRINCES
WHICH I SHOULD HAVE NO DIFFICULTY
WERE NOT TOO LARGE ❧ ❧ ❧
LOOK AT, BY REASON OF THE GREAT
THAT ONE IS OVERCOME BY THE SIGHT

SEEING   THE GRANDEUR OF ITS OF STONE, IS SUCH THAT, IT IS SAID, OF EUROPE COULD BE LODGED IN THEM, BELIEVING, PROVIDED THEIR RETINUES THIS ROYAL HOUSE IS SO AGREEABLE TO QUANTITY OF LITTLE TOWERS THEREON,

 Anonymous author, 1728

Text by Pierre Gascar
Translated from the French
by Richard Howard
Photographs by André Martin

CHAM

Collier-Macmillan Limited, London
The Macmillan Company, New York

All *rights reserved Copyright 1962 by*
Delpire Editeur. *Printed in France*

BORD

We often notice, in the environs of a château, provided it has some majesty and a certain renown, a kind of subservience in the landscape. The trees of the estate still conceal the structure from our sight, but already the last village, as we pass through it, dwindles and slumbers in a suspect peace redolent of dependency. In fields emptier than elsewhere, crops are prudently arranged in discrete acres of truck-garden produce. Over them, the silence of the feudal system, the silence that rises from the canvases of the early painters, from their pastoral background with its raw green or bluish horizon to the left, and in the distance a white structure showing the joints in its mortared stones. Doubtless we can discover in this silence of the pastoral background, besides the effacement and docility implied by the state of subordination, something quite close to stupor and even, as I should have said before remarking on its subservience, to an "astonishment" of the landscape.

The feeling of contrast shifts, sometimes, to the object, and just as the white squares of a chessboard are modified by the proximity of the black ones, independently of the phenomenon of opposition, so certain earthly realities—this village, these fields — can be subtly marked by the presence of a still invisible château, by its color, its form, and even by the intention it perpetuates. Later, we shall see if the contrary turns out to be true. I don't think so. Nothing is more docile, more sensitive than nature. In every case, our creations triumph over it. Chambord holds the landscape, in the oppressive sense of the word. A little more and all of the surrounding Sologne, beyond the woods that still conceal the château from view, would turn into the meager field hoed by a man the color of the earth, into the harsh green of a meadow sounding, by some mysterious correspondence, a note of deep melancholy, into the shabby woods. A little more and all Sologne would find, in humility, another season, another age, and would rejoin the images of an old order.

Here, this order is suggested everywhere: it is the suddenly straight road that follows the *allée* once crossing the wooded grounds and, at its end, the château which reveals itself, thrusting into the prospect a yellowish-white corner of a wall and, already above it, the clustered city of its pointed roofs, its turrets, cupolas, its stele-shaped chimneys. Nevertheless, the very mass of the structure, spreading as we

Left : West section
of the north front. Galleries connecting
the keep to the chapel tower

Right : East section of the north front.
On the second floor, the Queen's Chapel,
called the "Oratoire de François I,"
above two private stairways
leading down to the moat

*Right central
section of the south front,
southeast tower of the keep
from the terraces*

approach, impresses us first. As pale as if the stone had just been scraped, it retains the daylight, and moderates the occasional patches of shadow cast upon itself by its projecting sections. They are not extensive or emphatic enough to keep the impression of brightness from prevailing, to keep us from discovering, by an almost scholastic association of ideas, in these perforated and sculptured walls, the Renaissance in all its Italian brilliance and its exorcism of the darkness.

Thus everything would be readily resolved, and what we might earlier have suspected of being disturbing in the landscape: the black woods, the muddy fields, the mists off the Loire, would yield before this bright affirmation of intelligence and royalty.

But there are the roofs, the terraces—in a word, the whole upper part, so imposing, so luxuriant that in speaking of the walls and their pale luster, I have perhaps spoken only of the pedestal. This upper part of the château reveals itself better when we come from the hamlet whose old houses once served more or less as outbuildings.

From here, all we can see at first is what caps the château, raising it toward the sky, constructions not added to but traversing the building's mass like a range of organ pipes which appear only at a certain level, numerous and various structures, each of which possesses, though related to the style of the whole, an autonomous reality, so that it could, if detached and set in separate focus, stand for a pilaster, a votive pediment, a tower, a circular temple with columns. From a distance, if we avoid looking at the actual body of the building that is half hidden, moreover, by a dip in the terrain, these different elements of the upper part of the château suggest the disorder of an ancient city bristling with belfries that conceal each other as we move and finally permit a fluted cupola to appear, perforated by the whiter daylight of the arches.

At this level, bare branches forming a further lattice in front of this chaotic city of roofs darkened by applications and patches of slate, we can no longer speak of the light of the Renaissance, of a victory over the landscape. Quite the contrary. A little earlier, when we came by the road through the woods and when in the distance the château had not entirely emerged from the ground, this swarm of chimneys, of turrets, of campaniles, of domes supported by slender columns resembled the highest part of a grove of trees rising behind those that lined the way. Chambord reared into the sky a dense foliage topped by clumps of mistletoe, mingled with slender peaks, and a stone fleur-de-lis surmounting the château lantern topped this gigantic grove with a bough opening into a trident like the tip of a pinetree.

Northeast portion
of the central courtyard from the terraces.
In the center, the staircase of François I;
to the left, the colonnade connecting the staircase
to the keep. In the left foreground,
the apartments of François I

A city close at hand, a forest from a distance, this upper part of the edifice can thus, depending on the hour, the perspective, or the spectator's feelings, borrow the most unexpected shapes, and favor any illusion. Have I not, on occasion, as I approached the château of which I could see only the roofs, felt a vague fear, rather like what we suffer when we reach out toward some huge shellfish?

Do not charge me with an aberration, nor regard my feelings as an effect of the contagion which the madness of this building sustains. "One imagines oneself in the realms of Baghdad or Kashmir," wrote Alfred de Vigny. "A woman whose hair has been blown loose by the wind," said Chateaubriand, with neither more nor less exactitude. Had they lost their minds? Had the anonymous author who at the beginning of the eighteenth century, speaking of the château's famous double staircase, did not hesitate to assert: "There is a remarkable thing in this house, for the stairs are arranged in such wise that, if one seeks to go up to a room higher than the one in which one is, one must go down instead of up, which is a wonderful prodigy and difficult for those to believe who have not seen it for themselves"? Difficult to believe, indeed, yet none of these writers is raving. Everything is possible here. Better still, everything is true. Not, though, by the power of a spell, an enchantment whose workings we can never entirely divine or discover.

This upper part of the château, despite the diversity and distribution of the masses that compose it and that often constitute second thoughts, contrary impulses repressed just in time, bears witness to a pyramidal sense of construction. It is around the lantern surmounted by a fleur-de-lis, the highest point of the structure, that everything is organized, composed and, to a degree, in competition. Here each element strives against the next without ever entirely escaping the ascensional movement of the whole, which tends to this final point against the sky: this belvedere embellished with stained glass and so slender that no human being can ever creep into it, this stone nozzle bearing at its summit the revolute cross of the fleur-de-lis.

Speaking, a moment ago, of organ pipes to suggest this asymmetrical extrusion of oblong bodies beyond the lower mass, I regarded such an image as merely a way of describing a phenomenon of crystallization (the organ-pipe crystals of quartz) and did not suspect that this comparison would come to assume so much weight. There is, in fact, something quite close to musical composition in Chambord.

*Colonnade
and foot of the staircase
of François I*

Just as, in a symphony, each part tends to exist with an apparent autonomy, to demand attention, to monopolize both melody and emotion, whereas it draws the essentials of its power and intelligibility only from the whole in which it is included, each portion of this architecture, each chimney, each campanile, each of these motifs without specific destination rises, takes shape as if it were to be unique, to crown by itself the body of the structure and, reaching the ultimate point to which its energy takes it, stops only regretfully, exhausted, dismayed by the sky's immensity, its solitude, suddenly resigned to let others speak for it in the wind.

Whereupon the adjacent element takes over, asserts itself in its turn, with a greater strength, and manages to outstrip the one whose attempt had caught our attention

Cul-de-lampe *on a chimney shaft, on the southwest roof-terrace of the keep*

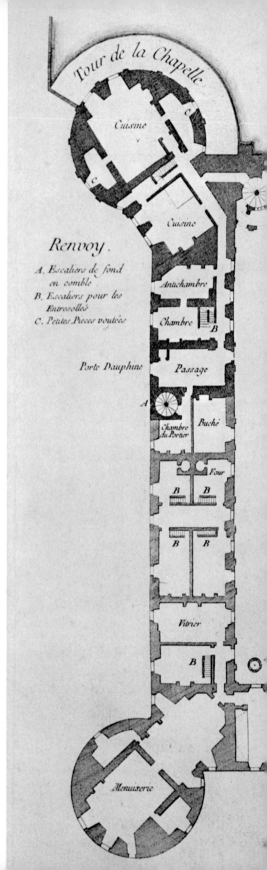

a moment ago. But soon it too stands motionless, its effort taken up immediately by another element which rises a little higher, and thus, by degrees, ordains the pyramidal whole. Still, it would not suggest music so much if, here and there, lapses of energy, gaps, the intrusion of forms elaborated out on another level, dissident motifs, did not provide those breaks in tone, those dissemblances without which we could not speak of harmony.

I am not sorry that this harmony is often a wild one, so that, violating the gravity of the whole, it combines, with a stone figure in wide pantaloons perched on a dome, something as pungent and tinkling as if the figure, one hand raised in a gracious gesture, were to begin turning, as in certain music boxes or mechanical toys.

This sign of frivolity, soon drowned in the character of the whole, would suffice by itself to date the château, and to localize the origin of those who conceived it. The figure I have just mentioned already belongs to Palladio, to Italy in any case.

There have been many attempts, and there will be many more, to find the name of Chambord's architect. For a long time it was believed to be Primaticcio. Some have even thought it was Leonardo da Vinci. The final plans were not drawn up until 1519, the year of Leonardo's death at Amboise, and actual construction did not begin until 1524, which at most would limit his participation to the elaboration of the initial plans. As for Primaticcio, he was only fifteen at the time. At the end of the last century, it was discovered in the archives that Domenico da Cortona, "le Bocca-dor," had worked on the château's plans, if he was not its only creator. Certain historians have, it is true, mentioned Vignola, Serlio, Il Rosso, and also several master masons from Blois whose participation is indisputable, without our knowing their specific contributions. Old documents mention Jacques Sourdeau, Pierre Trinqueau, and Jacques Coqueau, and wooden models of the edifice have been discovered in the houses of their descendants. Doubtless the title of "master mason" refers to these men, but it has been remarked that Jean Goujon himself bore no other. This historical point has, in fact, only a secondary interest. Chambord remains the expression of an art born on the other side of the Alps, and it matters little whether it is the result of an influence or of a transplantation.

A work of the Renaissance, then, but infinitely more complex, more disturbing, and, in a word, more magical than the works emanating, at this period, from the same Italian school. Doubtless the great movements of art do not exhibit a perfect uniformity, and include productions that are often hybridized, works in which the

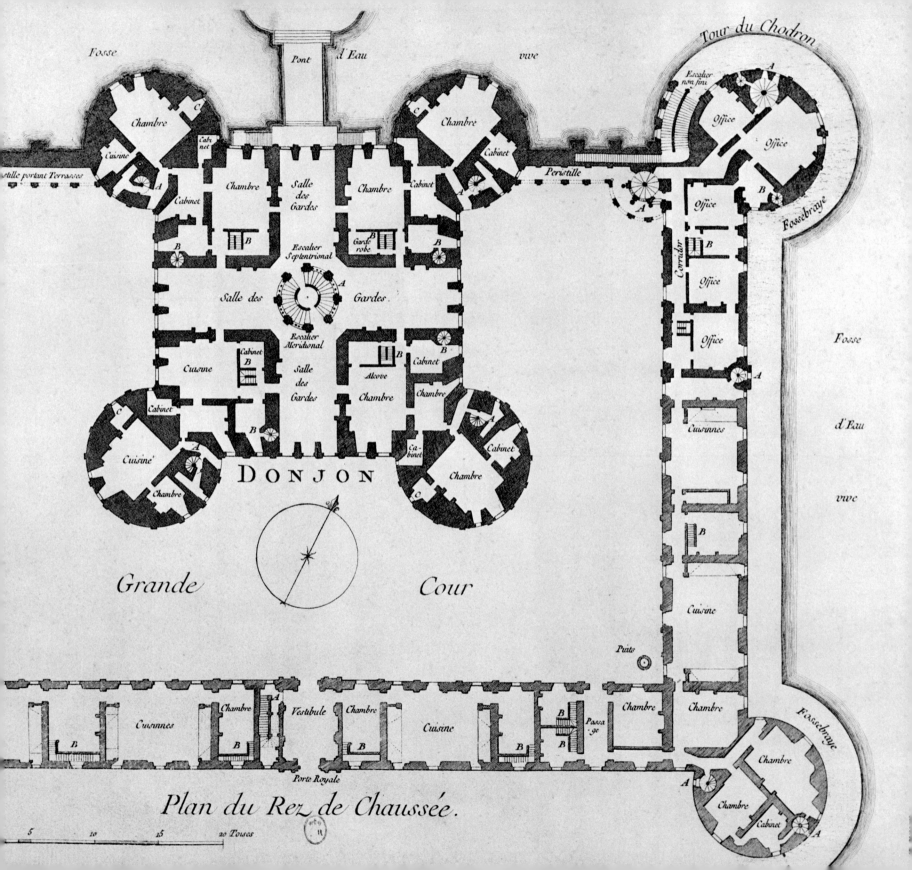

Fosse

Pont d'Eau vive

Tour du Chodron

Escalier
non fini

Chambre

Office

Office

C
Cabi
net

Cuisine

stille portant Terrasses

A

Cabinet

Chambre

Salle
des
Gardes

Chambre

Cabinet

Chambre

Cabinet

A

Peristille

B

A

B

Office

Fossebraye

B

B

Garde
robe

B

Corridor

Office

B

Escalier
Septentrional

B

A

Office

Salle des

Gardes.

Escalier
Meridional

Cabinet

A

Cuisne

Cabinet
B

Salle
des
Gardes

Alcove

B

Cabinet

B

Chambre

Cabinet

Fosse

Cuisinnes

d'Eau

C

Cabinet

A

A

Cabinet

vive

Cuisine

DONJON

Ca
binet

Chambre

A

C

B

Cuisine

Cuisine

Grande

Cour

Puits

Fossebraye

Chambre

Cuisinnes

A

Chambre

Vestibule

Chambre

B

B

B

Passa
ge

Chambre

Chambre

B

Cuisine

B

B

Chambre

B

Porte Royale

A

Cabinet

Plan du Rez de Chaussée.

5   10   15   20 Toises

Staircase of François I from the roof-terrace of the colonnade

in species which have undergone a biological evolution. Open, giving an impression of welcome—it is true that the inexpugnable whitness of the stone from the Cher hillsides, the Bourré stone of which the château is built, reinforces this sentiment—Chambord suggests nothing of the Middle Ages. That it has taken hold on the surrounding landscape, as I said before, that it "holds under its yoke" these woods, these fields, these villages there is no doubt, but less by the effect of its strength, its mass, as would have been the case two centuries earlier, than by the effect of its light and of its strangeness.

This strangeness of a great part of its elements has no visible origin. It apparently

Coffered cupola of the staircase of Henri II; the newel in the center

Pages 38 and 39 :
Top of the staircase of François I with its caryatids. On the left, gables surmounted by arched pediments projecting from the roofs of the galleries. On the right, apartments of François I.

37

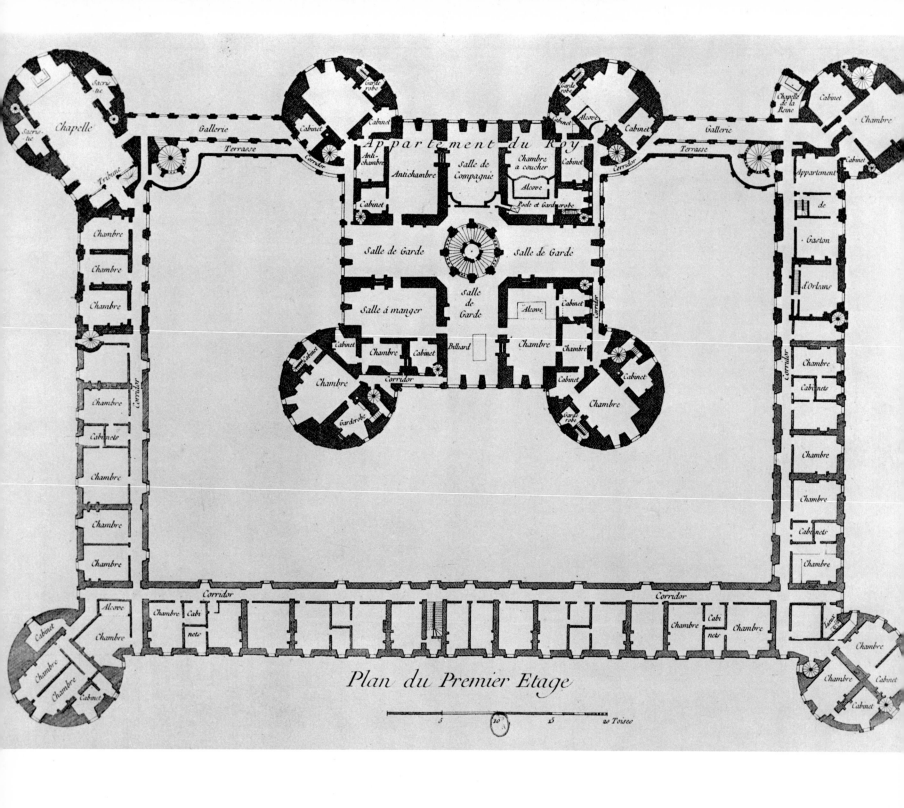

Plan du Premier Etage

Chapelle

Sacristie

Gallerie

Terrasse

Tribune

Chambre

Chambre

Chambre

Corridor

Chambre

Cabinets

Chambre

Chambre

Chambre

Alcove

Chambre

Cabinets

Chambre

Cabinet

Chambre

Chambre

Cabinet

Garde robe

Cabinet

Cabinet

Corridor

Appartement du Roy

Antichambre

Anti-chambre

Cabinet

Salle de Garde

Salle à manger

Salle de Garde

Salle de Compagnie

Chambre à coucher

Alcove

Poele et Garderobe

Cabinet

Salle de Garde

Alcove

Cabinet

Corridor

Chambre

Chambre

Cabinet

Billiard

Cabinet

Chambre

Corridor

Garderobe

Chambre

Cabinet

Chambre

Garde robe

Garde robe

Chambre

Chapelle de la Reine

Cabinet

Chambre

Gallerie

Terrasse

Appartement

de

Gaston

d'Orleans

Corridor

Chambre

Cabinets

Chambre

Chambre

Cabinets

Chambre

Chambre

Cabinet

Chambre

Corridor

Chambre

Cabi-nets

Chambre

Corridor

Chambre

Cabi-nets

Chambre

Alcove

Cabinet

Chambre

Chambre

Cabinet

Chambre

Chambre

Cabinet

5   10   15   20 Toises

Vault coffering
in the keep, with the emblems of François I :
the F surrounded by the girdle
of St. Francis of Assisi,
and the salamander

derives from a spontaneous creation, and reminds us that if all art lives by what it borrows from a preceding art, it is not always on the level of History as we know it that this continuity functions. Parallel to this history, exists a secret one, strewn with eccentric and unclassifiable facts and productions. It is in this shadowy filiation that Chambord takes its place, a work in which the spirit of the Renaissance is associated with a dateless esotericism somehow "floating in time" and constituting the second freedom of art.

Aware of the singular character of this edifice, and seeking an explanation for it, authors racked their brains to discover, within its purlieus, ritual symbols: the earlier rooms of the château might number 365 (the days of the year), the dimensions of the grounds might be seven leagues in length (the traditional seven). Futile speculations: the secret of Chambord is in each of us.

I have nonetheless been too inclined, up till now, to separate the edifice into two distinct parts: one forming the body of the building, the other including the whole chaos of towers, roofs, chimneys, campaniles, and the lantern around which these elements are grouped. The strangeness, the oneiric character, the marvelous dementia of this latter part finds an analogue, in another form, inside the château itself.

The double spiral staircase which from its inception has become the "curiosity" of Chambord (and I give the word here the meaning it has in the tourist guidebooks) serves as an axis to the keep, the great guardrooms which, on each floor, open in a Greek cross. The conception of this staircase has been interpreted as a caprice of the mind, the predilection for a *tour de force*, and perhaps such a view is correct. Yet this should not cause it to be considered as no more than one of those labyrinths to be found in country fairs. It has its appropriate and unmysterious anecdotes. As a child, the Grande Mademoiselle played here with her father, each laughing at being able, because of the double spiral, to go up or down without being seen by the other who nonetheless proceeded on the same level (actually, occasional apertures in the stairwell permit those on the stairs to see each other at certain moments).

Doubtless, we are affected by the elegance of this construction, by the grace and the individuality of the capitals that decorate it and offer, amid the intertwinings of a convolvulus or a budding honeysuckle, an angel's or animal's head swiftly carved and painted with the stupid stare of dead sheep; doubtless, we discover with

*Ceiling of the double-spiral
staircase of the keep, decorated with the emblems
of François I. In the center, the newel
containing the staircase leading to the lantern.
Around it,* culs-de-lampe *and colonnettes
surmounted by scallop shells*

some "apprehension" the hollowed core of this staircase— "medieval," historians call it, recalling that there already existed a model for it in the Bernardine monastery in Paris, but "Chinese" to me, for I sense, in this ingenuity, a spiritual atmosphere more suited to remote civilizations than to our own; yes, doubtless it is with a certain uneasiness that we measure the enormous height of this naked well whose summit is bathed in a churchly glow, while around this stone cylinder move, invisible...

Invisible: now we have come to it! I am rarely moved to mental representations of a historical nature. I avoid such imagery. Those, who, invisible to us standing at the bottom of this stairwell that resembles a factory chimney, now climb and descend the steps, blind to each other, may be wearing doublets, slashed pantaloons, swallow-tailed coats, the women in paniered gowns—we don't know, and it is of no moment.

What remains is this obscure movement, in the haste of secrecy, of confusion, or of betrayal: rival passing unseen rival, one mounting, the other descending, each running to her intrigue, her fortune, her revenge; what remains are these parallel yet contrary progressions of destinies: the mistress obliged to hurry down when "he's coming," when, taking the stairs two at a time, he tries to join her and, perhaps, from this moment, they can never again meet; what remains is this "irony of fate": the judge or statesman who slides one hand along the stone rail, holding in the other the document decreeing the ruin or death of a man, who along the other spiral, runs innocently about his business, glimpsing, through an aperture, a fold of a black cape, without thinking any more about it . . .

A staircase of deception, of absurd inadvertences, interlacing but adverse spirals . . . I shall be accused of being romantic. Behind this royal "stair-trap" of the Sunday visitors, I wanted to reveal the double vision of nightmare, of the dream, at least.

This dream, this *bizarrerie*, this love of the labyrinthine are to be found virtually everywhere inside the château, once we leave the great guardrooms opening onto the staircase. More naves than rooms, in fact, where the architects in charge of restoration, at the end of the last century, removed the flooring between the first and second floor, assuming that it did not exist in the château's initial plan.

In these halls—or these naves—we are still in the domain of traditional order and of majesty. The cofferings of the ceiling, once polychromed (or occasionally gilded: "Also those houses so highly prized. Panelled in enameled gold—Fontainebleau,

Chambour. . . '' wrote Ronsard), repeat the "F" of François I entwined in the Girdle of the Order of Saint Francis of Assisi, when they are not embellished with the salamander. But here, in these halls, that creature rarely emerges from the heraldic bestiary, and as a pacified symbol is content, as the King's motto has it, "to sustain the good and destroy the wicked."

Despite the reversible signification of fire, sometimes a defender, sometimes a destroyer, the moral remains clear, and it will take a long, solitary walk through the château, a persistent silence or a slight change in the light for the fabulous animal (as it is represented, for instance, on the vault of the staircase leading to the bedroom of François I, in an admirable *cul-de-lampe* attributed to Jean Goujon) to assert more of an intention, to participate in the mystery. This impression will be renewed among the capitals where the salamander, no longer exposed, or even a decorative object, overhangs a cornice, huddles in a corner, and becomes a "beast of the walls."

Other signs of the secret, faint at first, far between and ambiguous, as, in company, the expressions of persons linked by some complicity, appear among the some eight hundred capitals the structure includes. With the mythology of dolphins, sirens, dragons and satyrs are mingled above the Corinthian acanthus or the suppler vegetation that embellishes the architectural motifs of the period, heads of lions, of rams, of angels, and then, in a sudden impulse of realism, heads of men and, I am tempted to write, of the damned.

A damnation often imperceptible, being scattered, as I was saying. In order to fit into the capital's corner, the heads are flattened (into "knife blades," and perhaps to create an effect of perspective reestablishing the relief, the habitual fullness of the face, the mouths are distended into a wide oval. Rictus? What may seem infernal in the expression of these heads is reenforced by the way they emerge from the stone, suggesting that imprisonment in matter which is, especially in Dante, one of the forms of damnation. Few women; one, however, on one of the eight lower arches of the lantern, her face a little snub-nosed and, by the effect of the stone sheath, her naked, round breasts worked into cushions under her chin.

Will you follow me? I think I can regard these curiously tormented, awkward creatures as interesting ambassadors, and I shall even include in the lot several rather clumsily carved angels, afflicted with an old man's, corporation and a face illuminated with a wonderful falseness. Where will they lead us?

We have left the ingenious and royal staircase with its two spiral screws, the twelve great guardrooms arranged, on each floor, by fours in a Greek cross; we have left behind, in a word, all that architectural rigor which suggests, despite the abundance and the vivacity of ornaments, the chill of the diagram, a mechanism à la Leonardo da Vinci. The dream can be discovered here too, it is true, for there is a magic of classical geometry, a poetry and a perversion of geometry, but for the dream, our cicerones

*Detail of the south side
of the lantern. At this level,
the roof-terrace of the great staircase
of the keep forms a circular balcony
under the eight flying buttresses. At lower left,
pediment of a gable with pinnacles*

Interior of the lantern,
at the same level as the preceding picture.
In the center, the spiral staircase
leading to the summit

would say—if they existed—"for the dream, you have chiefly the corridors." The corridors, or as I should prefer to say, the passages. Once we penetrate the region where the apartments are, once we set foot in these parceled-out immensities, located on several different, constantly shifting levels and including some four hundred and forty rooms, no further orientation is possible, there are no landmarks: we are endlessly, from one place to the next, "reversed." Ten yards of gallery, two doors to pass through, a bedroom to cross, three yards of narrow corridor, a staircase to climb, a vestibule, a staircase down again, two rooms in succession, a closet at the far end of which opens a slit scarcely wider than the body, a bend, two steps, a door, and suddenly the vast pale daylight of an empty space, difficult to identify, with quadrangular mullioned windows: at the far end, another door, another corridor, another passage, more stairs. . .

Beyond the windows of the rooms we cross (soon hurriedly, nervously), the trees of the grounds, whose 13,590 acres are enclosed by a wall 32,808 yards long. Always the same, the trees, always the same, the forest pushing in front of it either a small stream, the Cosson, or, on the other side, the houses of a sleepy hamlet. Another labyrinth, the forest. Here, inside the château, all that remains, then, is to exhaust the premises. But getting lost in this endless succession of rooms, corridors, vestibules, and stairs, getting hot-tempered or getting hysterical changes nothing: we come up against emptiness. Everything is almost dead, for the moment, the secret is scarcely alive now, and the carved figures leaning forward in the gloom look like the kind on dried-up fountains that weakly exhale the stale stench of wells.

But before trying to revive this secret, before considering the various perspectives that History affords Chambord, perhaps it would be a good idea to recall that this château, this creation at once so alive and so funereal, so welcoming and mysterious, luminous and dim, rational and obsessed, is above all the realization of a dream.

It has often been asserted that Chambord, like several other châteaux of the same period, served as a model for Rabelais who, moreover, quotes its name in *Gargantua* for his abbey of Thélème. The resemblance between Chambord and Rabelais's imaginary edifice appears, in fact, at many points of the chapter devoted to the description of the abbey. Here are the round towers "having an extent of sixty paces in diameter"; here the staircase that "rose to above the roof itself and there ended in a pavilion"; here the "figures of little mannequins and animals of all kinds," and so on. Hence it cannot be denied that Rabelais borrowed something from the architecture of his time in conceiving his abbey. Yet this does not keep Chambord and Thélème from being parallel creations, by which I mean that they translate the same desire, belong to the same dream. This dream is the Renaissance's craving for the marvelous, a need as old as man, of course, and already expressed in the art of the Middle Ages, but henceforth through the intermediary of a philosophy of happiness.

Advocating an abandonment of austerity, which, however, does not mean the abandonment of all morality, since it is based on the belief that human nature tends toward virtue, beyond constraint, proposing a liberation likely to favor a spiritual gain, this new philosophy, in its broad outlines, rejoins classical Epicurism. Despite this suspect reference, it wins over religious minds, inspires Coquillard to write his *Droits nouveaux*, Jean Le Maire de Belges his *Temple de Vénus*, and to Rabelais dictates the famous formula of Thélème: *"Faye ce que vouldras"* (Do what you will).

Invited to a kind of earthly Eden, human beings would be purified upon contact with beauty, and draw closer to God by happiness. These projects of an ideal life, whose different aspects it would take too long to examine here, if they first expressed the desire to recover a naturalness hitherto repressed by the moral corset of Catholicism, constituted, until the corset was loosened, a flight into the marvelous.

Thélème is a philosophical proclamation and, at the same time, just such a flight into the marvelous. Chambord, which a Venetian ambassador compared, at this time, to the "abode of Morgan Le Fay and of Alcina," is also the result of a dream. In what I should call "the desperate refinement of this château" appears—limited here, by the resistance, the inertia of matter—the delirium of beauty which, in the description of Thélème, calls from Rabelais's pen the words porphyry, serpentine, chalcedony, Numidian marble, and makes him speak of golden figures, alabaster fountains, "mirrors of crystal set in fine gold frames embellished with pearls."

Conceived in an unconscious desire for unreality, at least, this transcendence of reality, image of an impossible happiness, Chambord, down through the centuries, will not lose its faltering purity, its wavering whiteness, a place of shadows where the light—the greatest light of man's dreams—never vanishes altogether.

These shadows of "Subhistory" approach us now. We sink into them, in the labyrinth once more. The complication of the place, the arrangement of the premises that seems improvised, derives from no *esprit de géométrie* : door upon door, corridor rejoining a remote gallery after a hundred turns and getting a little lost along the way, cutting off vestibules, spiral staircases, obscure passages that lead to forgotten rooms, this labyrinth corresponded, some historians say, to the choice expressed by François I when, in his thirtieth year, he ordered the château to be built. So many meanders favored the secrecy of lovers' meetings.

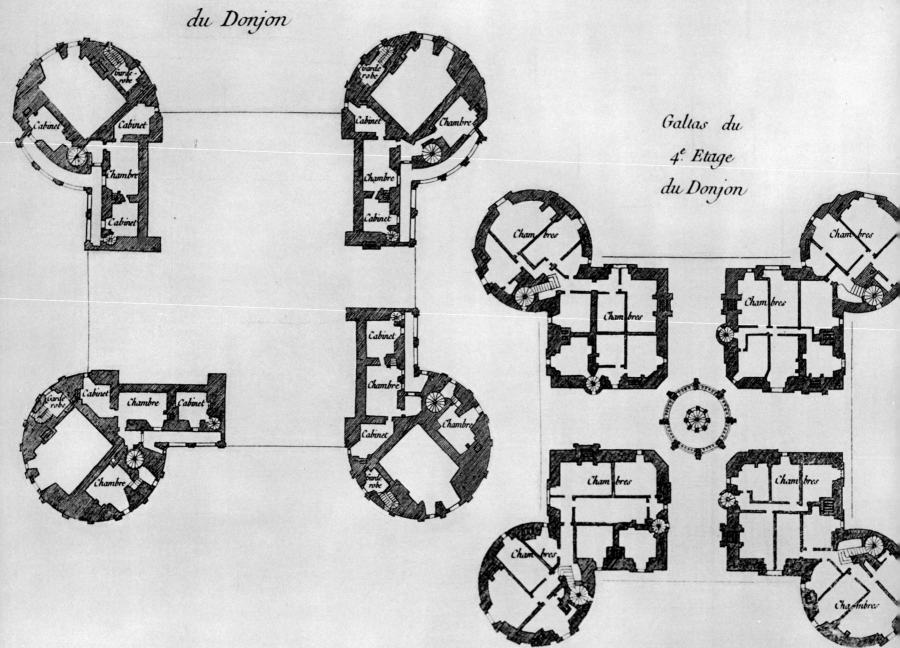

Entresolles du

Second Etage

du Donjon

Galtas du

4.ᵉ Etage

du Donjon

Cabinet

Cabinet

Garde-robe

Chambre

Cabinet

Garde-robe

Chambre

Cabinet

Cabinet

Chambre

Cabinet

Garde-robe

Cabinet

Chambre

Cabinet

Chambre

Cabinet

Chambre

Garde-robe

Chambres

Chambres

Chambres

Chambres

Chambres

Chambres

Chambres

Chambres

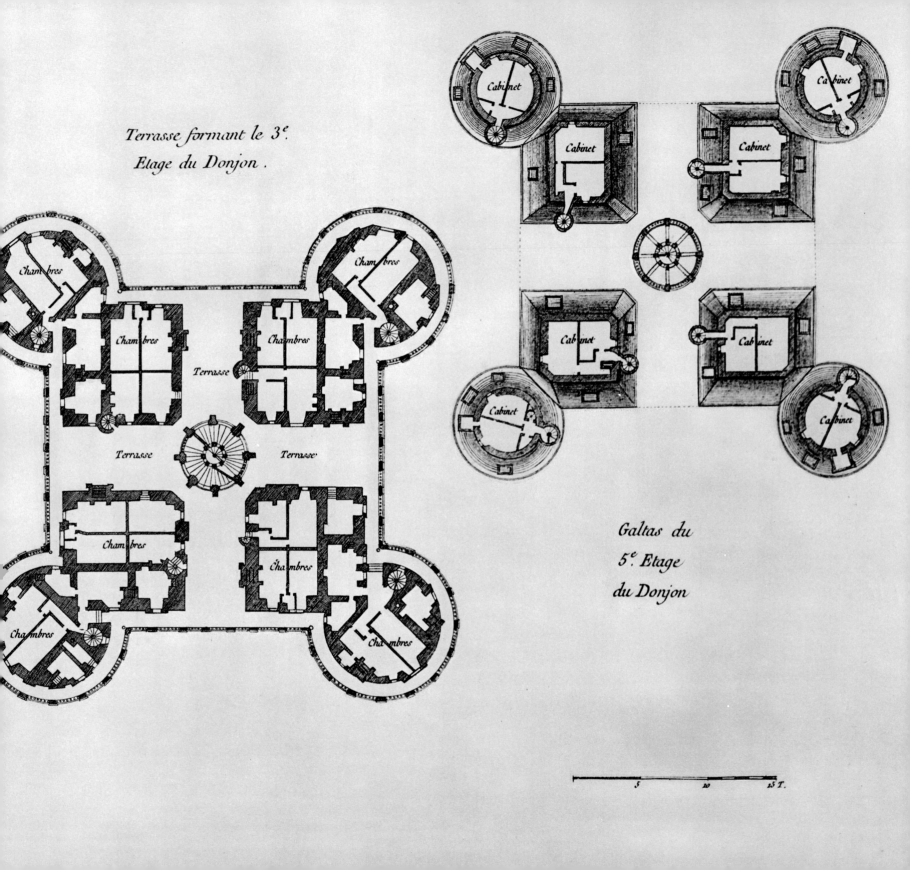

Terrasse formant le 3ᵉ.
Etage du Donjon.

Chambres

Chambres

Chambres

Chambres

Terrasse

Terrasse

Terrasse

Terrasse

Chambres

Chambres

Chambres

Chambres

Cabinet

Cabinet

Cabinet

Cabinet

Cabinet

Cabinet

Cabinet

Cabinet

Galtas du
5ᵉ Etage
du Donjon

5   10   15 T.

world was blackened." And finally, to skip Stanislas Leczinski and Queen Marie, who spent eight uneventful years at Chambord, kind and pious and speaking to the peasants, as in Rousseau, we come to the Maréchal Maurice de Saxe and with him a great shadow, as we shall see later.

Toward the end of his life, he sometimes gathered in his bedroom, in the evening, certain women and lackeys. There was laughter and drinking. What followed can be guessed. No doubt the image that rises here is not so unexpected: the eighteenth century, its licentiousness—but wait! All this happens deep in the black labyrinth of the château where the wind, sucked up by the monumental staircase, by the twelve other great staircases (which often have an axis carved to imitate a twisted sheet), by the infinity of those not immediately apparent, led along the galleries, the corridors whose thousand doors creak, has made short work of the rare candles in the passageway. Outside, everywhere, night lies over the woods, the imprisoning, utter darkness. Let eroticism (and the worst kind) be a revenge, then. But everything, here—and since the beginning—is a revenge! Now we must return to the terraces, at the foot of the city of the roofs, the campaniles, the chimneys, the towers. The ornamental profusion of the edifice clearly testifies to a need for affirmation, for a victory whose political character first leaps to the eyes. Through the eroticism of the whole, there appears in the countless fleur-de-lis, the windows surmounted with crowns, the emblems, and that F.R.F. (François Roi de France) in slate letters on one chimney shaft, as though crudely stenciled, an ostensible sign and stubborn proclamation of royalty.

Less than a century after the Hundred Years' War, court life not yet having suppressed the ambitions of the nobles, royalty realized its precarious and threatened position. The sun of Louis XIV, which appears discreetly here and there (the places where the stone remained clear had become infrequent, it is true), will constitute, on the other hand, the image of maturity, of serenity. It is in this political tension of the Renaissance that we discover the medieval trace we would seek in vain (apart from a few details) in the château's aspect. Deep in the woods, in the middle of an uncertain and still quite empty France, the château of Chambord, behind the delirium of its roofs, the grace of its ornaments, the light of its façades, retains its essential cruelty. We cannot deny that in some places love's frenzy is expressed, asserted. And so is that of the chase.

If, in creating Chambord, François I intended to bring himself closer to a woman he had an inclination for, he also desired to build a hunting lodge. Like the Bois de Boulogne and the Bois de Bussy, between which rose the Pavillon de Montefrault that had belonged to the Comtes de Blois, the surrounding plains, sandy and humid, were—and are, even today—peopled by game. In the special psychology of the period, the hunt readily "intermingles" at this junction of reason, humanism, and the shadow of the medieval. The prey becomes, quite often, ambiguous.

Gables and chimneys
on the northeast part of the keep roof terrace.
On the far right, a flying buttress
of the lantern

Yet we must not anticipate; for a royalty still unsure of itself, the chase may first appear as a passable substitute for war, and the king

> *Sets off to hunt in the woods, spear in hand,*
> *Without dogs, to show his tender mistress*
> *He is as bold as he is fair...*

"Imitating" these lines by Ronsard, Charles IX, in the woods of Chambord, one day runs down a stag, alone, without a pack or any huntsmen. No doubt there is already something sinister in all this, and d'Aubigné must have felt it, writing of this same king:

> *A suspect mother...*
> *Made him take the blood of beasts...*
> *His wild youth...*
> *Was all of blood, and its pleasure*
> *To kill without mercy the moaning stags...*

The glades of Chambord lead to the Wars of Religion and to another blood, in the darkness. But despite so much darkness, we are still, here, in legible history.

Chambord also belongs, as I was saying, to another, secret history, whose elements are witchcraft and terror. The year 1533 was one of pestilence. In 1535, amid proscriptions, arrests, tortures—for the first manifestations of the spirit of the Reformation must be put down—there occurred, in Paris, the procession of expiation, in which the King was seen walking, a candle in his hand. Terror still surrounded the death of the Dauphin, poisoned by a certain Montecuccoli who was drawn and quartered by four horses under the eyes of the Court. And terror would never again be far way, following this uninterrupted cortege of the dead: Henri II, his eye and brain pierced by a lance thrust; François II, buried at sixteen; Charles IX at twenty-four...

All this happens not only at Chambord, of course, but what forebodings, what fears do the survivors not bring with them to these premises? What oblivion do they not seek in the pleasures of love and the violences of the chase, at the risk of finding here, along with a brief revenge, a surfeit of malediction? If the hunter's curse belongs, the world over, to legendary morality, it is because the hunt represents man's desperate quest, a blind flight into blood. All other flights are, so to speak, comprised in this one, and here we must quote, in this regard, some passages of that mid-sixteenth-century song "Marguerite of the White Doe," in which the terrible ambiguity of the hunt is summarized with disturbing simplicity :

I am a girl by day   *To skin the white doe for us!*
And by night a white doe   *And the skinner answers,*
The hunt is upon me   *"What can I say to this?*
The barons and the princes...   *She has the fair hair*
Upon the third attempt   *And the breast of a girl."*
The white doe is taken.   *Drawing out his knife*
Let us ask the skinner   *He quickly quartered her...*

At the same time, for here we enter a kind of cynegetic mythology sustained by fear, by the medieval solitude and its chaotic metaphysics, there develops the theme of the *Wilde Jagd* of the Germans or of the *"chasse démoniaque"* that we find in Ronsard, in a passage of the *"Hymne des Daimons"* :

I heard, meseemeth, a howling hunt
Of dogs that followed my path, step by step,
I saw, behind me, on a great black horse,
A man that looked to be all of bones...

Here Ronsard returns—but perhaps he had found it himself?—to a legend proper to Chambord, though it too belongs to the vast myth of the *Wilde Jagd* and the "black huntsman" I have just referred to. Near the Pavillon de Montfrault, which the Château de Chambord was to replace, grows "the grass that deranges." He who treads on it by night soon meets, in the woods, a hunter dressed in black and accompanied by black dogs. This is Thibault, Comte de Blois, also called "The Old Man" or—God knows why—"The Trickster." Since his death, he returns to haunt the woods every night, at the head of his pack. No one knows what he seeks. It varies, according to the popular imagination, and it is quite possible, as certain historians collecting the oral traditions suggest, that "The Old Man" also leads, on occasion, those aerial hunts whose echoes, down through the centuries, generations of peasants, in their sleeplessness, have thought they heard over their roofs...

Thus, in the spirit of Chambord, there functions, without any doubt, a secret presence—and why not say a remorse—of the chase. This presence is attested by

*Ordonnance of a gable
from the wing of François I.   Mullioned
window framed by a sill, pilasters,
and a stone and slate entablature,
surmounted by an arched pediment
crowned with fleurs-de-lis.*

figures of animals peopling the capitals of the structure. That the initial object of this representation has long since been transcended and that it has become the expression of a remorse doubtless remains to be proved. All that matters is to remember that around Chambord the nocturnal persistence of "The Old Man," "The Trickster," symbolizes the quest for the ever-elusive prey, or the prey which, miraculously captured and struck down, changes shape before your eyes and escapes you still, abandoning you to a new sin. I know that this kind of "bad dream" of the hunt fades if we shift our attention to the great beats of the time of Louis XIV who, on several occasions, sojourned at Chambord where Molière first performed *Le Bourgeois gentilhomme* (in one of the great halls of the keep, we can still see the hooks that held up the stage curtain). There is something here that at first glance doesn't follow "the direction of the shadows," but I have already remarked the different aspects, the alternations appropriate to this place.

Thus I do not consider it excessive to link to the supernatural qualities of the sixteenth century, so apparent in the history, literature, and art of the period, a certain somber tonality of Chambord, a tonality perceptible not only in facts or legends but in the very appearance of the château, where in certain lights—before the rain, in the evening, or on winter days— some of the chief elements reveal a cruel and funereal character or allow a kind of melancholy peasant ruggedness to appear.

I am thinking, on the other hand, of those high stele-shaped chimneys, those pilasters darkened by inlaid slate or often bearing, in the form of a blind half-dormer, the carved, curving garlands, the limp ornamentation that we find in full bloom, at the end of the eighteenth century, in the sullen art of Saint-Sulpice and the Panthéon. I am also thinking of those heavy corner towers, sole medieval vestige, traditional symbol of suzerainty, which in France were not to disappear altogether until the seventeenth century, those towers capped with a heavy slate roof on whose summit the campanile reveals, from inside, the crude framing of a farm dovecote. Here is the shadow's share: the shadow that awaits the hunter, in the woods, at twilight, and will soon fill with apparitions, the shadow of all fears, the shadow that will stretch over France for the thirty-five years of the Wars of Religion. These will come close enough to Chambord for the village priest to be stabbed, one day, at the altar.

Yet I cannot repeat often enough that this contrast—on one side, the light of the

Chimneys.
In the foreground,
decorative pinnacles on
a gable pediment.

Renaissance, on the other, the shadows of the secret— remains, at least in this simple formulation, quite arbitrary, especially since I have not yet given light the place which is its due, since I have not spoken of its own mysteries.

This juxtaposition of two tones, opposed in essence if not always in actuallity, nonetheless marks Chambord more than any other creation of this period. It would be futile to seek equivalents in other works of art, but upon close examination, do we not find something close to the diversity of Ronsard, in whom we often continue to see only an Anacreontic poet, despite his various accents of philosophical melancholy?

The Latin freedom—or the Italian grace— the profusion of mythological references, an undeniable *"gentillesse française"* (thus, seen from another point of view, the simplicity of the slate-capped towers, the unadorned dovecotes of nobles suddenly combined with a strange perversion of colors and forms, with fear, with the preposterous and exotic aspect of this Renaissance, not in the luster of lacquer but in the stones of the Cher hillsides, the stone of cemeteries, and the silence of Sologne. Sometimes at the heart of a poem, we find these disturbing accents in Ronsard, "that secret darkest in the darkness of men's minds" of which d'Aubigné spoke later.

Here we are trapped in a coil of correspondences, and if the preceding one can be verified as to the mind's content, it does not seem very clear with regard to that mind's form. If we wanted to find, in the literature of the period, an image of Chambord's complication, of what, for lack of another term, I shall call its "baroque," it is perhaps in Maurice Scève that we must seek it, in one of those poets occasionally sliding into amphigory and preciosity from an excess of exigence and sincerity (for the sincerity of literature is in metaphor).

At many points, Chambord's architecture is metaphorical or, at least, caught in a sequence quite close to that of dialectics. Here everything occurs on the vertical level, since the impulse toward pyramidal construction dominates and provokes that multiple explosion above the main bodies of the structures and terraces. All this wild external ornamentation is arranged from the bottom upward.

Here we are confronted with the dialectic of boxes that endlessly emerge from each other, or collapsible spyglasses, and we discover in it a habitual mechanism of the mind, at the level of the subconscious. To be convinced of this, it is enough to reproduce in isolation, with a pencil, the shape of any one pilaster chosen at random, an experiment I have already made. The movement of our fingers holding the pencil becomes immediately mechanical. The column's motifs succeed each other, flowing naturally out of each other, without our thinking about it, as when, listening to someone on the telephone, we draw on a sheet of paper some barbarous, endlessly complex geometrical figure. Yet without regarding this as one of the abysses of the psyche's activity, we cannot deny that this innocent pastime constitutes a revenge in solitude and a perversion of our silence. Revenge in solitude, perversion of silence,

Cupola of a staircase.

Pages 70 and 71 :
Chimneys and gables
on the northwest side of
the keep roof terrace

perhaps there is, in these two formulas, a beginning of the definition of art, at least of the art of Chambord, profoundly individual as it is, despite the mark of the Italian school, and forever separated from an art that is medieval, religious, and thereby social.

Undoubtedly this free expression is based on the classical order which the Renaissance restored to its place of honor. In this pilaster, in this column that separates itself from the mass at a certain height, an architect could indicate the gorgerin, the volute, the upper and lower torus, just as at any point of the construction he could point to entablatures, architraves above Corinthian columns, Roman arches, composite or Ionic capitals, a thousand stock and, in a sense, pacified elements.

The present miracle, the miracle of Chambord (and, to generalize, the miracle of art, often enough) is not achieved, however, by the accumulation or the fusion of styles but, rather, by the control and modulation of each of them. Not being an architect, I cannot say at which moment, between a certain abacus and a certain astragal, we may situate a history which is entirely unexpected and long, very long. It triumphs, in every case, it absorbs the classical motifs which surround it and which manage to recover their arrangement only at the moment the architectural specialist passes, these motifs then suggesting those men of a priori sound mind mistakenly confined in an asylum who rush to the barred window when a visitor appears and indicate their presence by rational remarks, though unable, all the same, to keep their voices from being already altered by the contagion of madness.

By thus emphasizing the share of baroque accumulation to be found at Chambord, I should be in danger, if the photographic illustrations of this book were not here to complete my reflections, of affording a notion of entanglement, of seething interiorization, rather than a notion of energy and impulse. Yet, I repeat, the château's movement remains specifically ascensional. This movement is sustained by the slenderness of the masses, the extremely oblong form of the windows, the abundance of columns, the areas of almost bare stone arranged between the ornaments of the base and those of the summit.

These bare spaces, this abrupt and deliberate return to austerity, has something implacable about it and also affords the somewhat funereal note to which I have already referred. No matter: we rise, we climb, and come up against the sky which flees (it is rare that the sky of Sologne is motionless) this array of peaks and crests releasing,

in a kind of thin, tenuous whisper, the copious murmur of the stones and of History.

Asphyxiating purity: not much is left, at this height, of actions, of words. The carved figures standing against the sky, these personages—and the angels themselves— which we had thought, from below, capable of turning, of pivoting to some unheard music, are arrested forever and stand, one arm bent, before eternity, with upon them, in epaulettes, in cuffs, in ribbons, a greedy moss that nonetheless thickens year after year: the leprosy of silence.

And not far from them, interminable rectangular chimneys, various steles inlaid with black lozenges, endlessly rising to this level, topped with triangles of stone and aligned side by side, saw-teeth inverted and placed one behind the other, sharp battlements wheeling to constitute a crest in depth, a dense defense and, this time, I imagine, whistling cruelly in the wind.

Sometimes, just before the end of this rush to the heights which elongates a mullioned window, the need is felt, above the last entablature, for two buttresses which manage to raise, on a platform bulging into a cupola, three little figures worn by bad weather, naïve, touching after so much erosion, and guarded by the great stone vases, seeming to represent the Holy Ampulla, that appear a little lower down.

Lingering over these various elements, I constantly turn, with that sincere yet deliberate indifference which "crowning glories" sometimes inspire in me, around the finial piece of the structure: the great central lantern that, amid these countless constructions, various but almost always enigmatic, speaks the language of an expected solemnity. Temple, perforated sanctuary, embellished with stained glass, this is, in its own ways, the "dome" (in the sense, too, of *duomo*, an Italian cathedral).

Eight huge buttresses forming Roman half-arches and curving over the same number of columns suggest this dome. Rich in volutes, two minor lanterns superposed, the last topped with the fleurs-de-lis, carry nearly eleven feet above the terraces this construction whose majesty first seems of religious inspiration. And it is here that there occurs, to my eyes, a marvelous mental audacity, touching on the absurd and affording one of the keys to Chambord: anywhere in the world, this huge and sumptuous lantern, this dome suggested by the buttresses and the volutes would cap the apse of a church, or at least a tomb, even the great hall of Parliament, a palace.

In the foreground,
upper section of a chimney.
On the right, pinnacles decorating
a chimney shaft.

Here it simply covers a staircase, the famous double spiral staircase around which, in stories, the keep is disposed.

If we forget the simultaneously poetic and historic significance of Chambord, we are struck by the extremely gratuitous character of this château which, in a spirit of realism, we can reduce to a brilliant stylistic exercise. Ruinous to maintain on account of its dimensions, its structure, and the abundance of its ornaments, difficult to heat, despite its 365 chimneys, for the staircases open to the outer air—such as the staircase of François I and that of Henri II—as well as the long galleries, favor a constant circulation of air, the edifice is regarded by all sensible architects as virtually uninhabitable. "God keep any honest man from ever living in a house built by Primaticcio!"

Finial of a chimney, the flues in the form of a fleur-de-lis.

Decorative element attached to the side of a chimney

exclaimed Paul-Louis Courier apropos of Chambord (which he attributed incorrectly to Primaticcio). This inhospitality of the premises led the various occupants, except for the first ones, who were accustomed to living with cold stone (only tapestries woven of colors to match those of the season covered the walls of the bedroom of François I) to withdraw increasingly to the innermost part of the château, and there to construct a habitation to man's measure.

After Louis XIV, who saw to the inner construction of a part of the first floor of the keep, other spaces, in the eighteenth century, were divided into ever smaller apartments until the builders finally achieved that bedroom of the Maréchal de Saxe, dim and closeted, like the one we would have found, at the period, in any house in the Rue des Fossés Saint-Jacques in Paris: the lair, the refuge.

So that we are back at the point where we were, a moment ago, when I was describing Maurice de Saxe trying to warm his blood by the spectacle of the amorous frolics of his entourage, while beyond the walls of his room reigned the enormous void of the château and the night. History, Subhistory, once again. In its anecdotic form, it reminds us that everything here was not solitude. The Maréchal had brought one of his regiments to Chambord, and the principal entrance was guarded by fifty men, among them those singular black uhlans mounted on white horses.

Inside the structure functioned a numerous domestic staff including not less than thirty-five *officiers de bouche* (officials who served at the King's table). In addition, visits of actors (among them, the young Madame Favart) coming to perform plays and, from time to time, the arrival of a "netful" of court ladies—according to the Maréchal's own expression— ready to amuse the officers for whom residence at Chambord was wearisome. These diversions occurred among Gobelins and Savonnerie tapestries, among precious furniture on which stood cups by Cellini, the Carracci, Giovanni da Bologna, faïences by Bernard Palissy, enamels by Petitot.

Yes, but one day in October, 1749, Maurice de Saxe writes: "Chambord is a hospital. I have more than 300 sick, many dead, and the rest have the faces of those risen from the dead." The Maréchal himself was to die a year later, not, as has sometimes been thought, of a wound received in a duel, but from a chill and also, apparently, from a moral breakdown: Chambord was truly uninhabitable.

I do not mean to make a pretext of the end—both wretched and yet with a certain grandeur— of this baffling personage (in order to escape the boredom of Chambord, had he not planned, among other things, to gather the Jews in one part of the French territories in America and to become their king?) to defend the thesis of a curse weighing on this château. I am merely tempted to show that this royal construction, one of the first linked to the affirmation of the monarchy and one of the most brilliant at its initiation, was rapidly abandoned, forgotten, and doomed. But this historical failure accords it a place in another order: the order of the human and the secret.

*Chimney shafts,
staircase cupolas, and towers.
In the background, lantern
of the chapel tower*

We have virtually no detailed documents as to the past of this château, on account of the marginal situation it occupied for centuries, but each time that the dark veil covering this past parts, it is a beam of burning truth that reaches us: François I, the women in the naked stone, and the echoes of the *Wilde Jagd;* Charles IX and, in the Bois de Bussy, all the blood of the Wars of Religion; the Grande Mademoiselle and her belated love (a seventeenth century print shows the gullied vicinity of the château, under a heavy sky, and for some reason I connect her passions—as well as those of the Renaissance—to this deep *grisaille*); Maurice de Saxe, finally. . . .

Behind this, History as we conceive it, the History of the historians, fades away. Nothing is left, between long silences, great gaps, except a few bare, isolated facts. From the Maréchal de Saxe to the Revolution: nothing, a Marquis de Polignac. In 1793, a commissioner was appointed to remove from the château all fleur-de-lis and all insignia of royalty. There were too many: he gave up. The château became, for a time, a remount depot. Which is no reason to assume vandalism, sacrilege. All solitudes are alike. The long walls of Chambord, if we glance down at the bottom of the structures, can assume, at certain moments, the precise color of the walls bordering those remount pens, and thereby recover the lighting of our story.

The Convention put up for auction all the precious Renaissance objects the château contained and made still emptier this enormous empty muricated shell (the kind with many spines). Napoleon planned, for a while, to have the château restored, and no doubt we should be glad that he shrank from the expense, for his taste in buildings was bad. He gave the château to Maréchal Berthier, a dull-witted man who applied his initials, subsequently scratched out, over the fireplaces, and felled a great deal of timber, from which he made a great deal of money. In a word, a vacuum.

Chambord more or less returned to official History during the Restoration, one of the most banal and boring periods France has known. Servility toward the royal family inspired a certain Comte de Calonne to offer to the newborn son of the late

Comte de Berry the château which a British colonel had acquired a short while before. A national subscription covered the expenses of the transaction.

A few liberals got excited, among them Paul-Louis Courier: "Twelve thousand acres of land put to the plow would be worth more than twelve thousand acres devoted to a rich man's pleasure ground. . . ." Further, did not the memories linked to Chambord risk corrupting the youth of the Duc de Bordeaux, once he was out of his swaddling clothes? All the other arguments contained in the pamphlet, which was to earn Courier two months in prison, are of a similar nature. The pretensions of the monarchy awakened only the grudges of a practical-minded bourgeois who would have voted for the destruction of Chambord, if he had had the chance, and who by an understandable antiroyalism became the lawyer of the "black band," that society of speculators who bought unused châteaux and churches for demolition.

The nineteenth century passed over Chambord, saved in the end, perhaps, by this national subscription, and become the seat of legitimism, without leaving any other marks upon it than two monogram weathervanes, a graffito cut by the Duchesse de Berry inside the lantern, and the traces, on the outer walls, of the shots exchanged by the units of Chanzy's army and the Prussians, in 1871. Subsequently, the presence of the Comte de Chambord appears only as a dim dream and does not restore the château to History—from which, as we have seen, it early became detached.

Perhaps as a result of its isolated geographical situation, forgotten in a region full of charm but hardly cheerful, often entirely abandoned ("So lovely a place to be left to perish in wretchedness," writes the author of *Délices de la France* in 1728), Chambord has not acquired the legendary prestige belonging to other structures, often less imposing and less beautiful, which inspires an almost religious respect.

As for the history of the secret to which the château belongs, rare, as we know, are those who risk exploring it or who, at least, divine its existence. Transfixed in its enigmatic splendor, virtually cut off from the past, mute or speaking to only a few, Chambord comes close to inspiring, even in those who admire it and make their pilgrimages to it with pleasure, the feeling of freedom and ownership that one can feel only in the presence of a thing entirely public, entirely "surrendered" or abandoned.

In no place in the world, probably, can one see so many graffiti. They rise upon

Dice of the ordonnance
of a small lantern surmounting
a staircase cupola

Pages 84 and 85 :
The château from the southeast.

the walls to a surprising height, sparing none, creeping along the lintels, extending into the window recesses, running under your hand along the bannisters, the balconies. Whatever their origin, their age, they constitute, by their very abundance, a kind of calligraphic monument applied to the original one, adopting its forms, its every meander.

Like those myriad tiny molluscs that cover old shells or, better still, the hulls of ships lying on the sea's bottom for centuries, they form a crust (in fact, millions of tracks, of prints, a protective veneer that defends these premises from death).

We are, though, within our rights to resent a "Dudule et Ginette Lacroix 1959" incised (with the help of a nail file, I suppose) under a certain *cul-de-lampe* bearing winged horses or sirens and dated 1549. Yet even here I see, in this absurd inscription, another stage in the eternity of these stones, a form of life, extremely vulgar but as effective, as certain, as comforting as the tawny flesh of the tiny periwinkle that we have just detached from an age-old coral. Parasitism, insult doubtless, but at a certain pitch of solitude, there is scarcely any other way for what is "underneath" to send out new branches. The spring of the graffiti covers the tender stone of Chambord, covers it so well, with a web so dense, that on the outside walls the old inscriptions, already three-quarters effaced by the weather, give it a rather gentle surface, the surface texture of gypsum.

It happens, moreover, that the tradition of graffito was founded, here, by the least contestable authorities (I mean, least contestable in the eyes of the majority of visitors). I have already mentioned the too-famous distich of François I scratched on a windowpane ("*la donna mobile*" that the refrain was to take over). Of this same king, so lavish in mottos, another inscription is shown, in the recess of a bay window, inside the bedroom he is said to have occupied during his numerous sojourns. Here it is a question of a complete sentence. We do not know if it is apocryphal (the handwriting has the angular quality of the period), in any case it is illegible: a vague scolopendra among the swarm of "Dudule-bugs," these latter precise and clearly dated. More venerated (doubtless because she happened to be in the opposition and

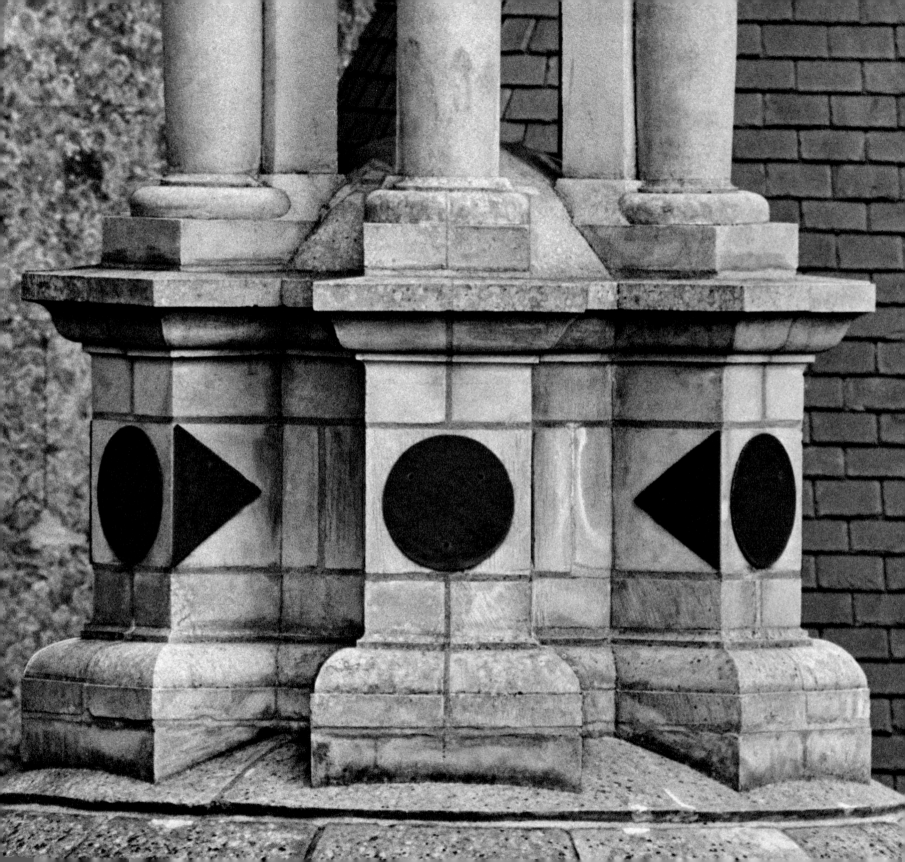

The château from the northwest.
In the foreground, the chapel tower.
On the right, wing of Henri II

Pages 88 and 89 :
North front of the château from the
Rond Point Saint-Louis

enjoyed the halo of royal outlaws), Marie-Caroline de Bourbon, Duchesse de Berry, was entitled, for her graffito, to a little emblazoned zinc box that, attached to the wall, has rescued it from subsequent sacrilegious hands. We may, of course, prefer as vestiges of remote periods, the scribbling, the clumsy and vain calligraphy of the lackeys and guardsmen who passed through these premises. Very early dates abound, in these inscriptions: those of the seventeenth and eighteenth centuries, sometimes intertwined with names which only historians could recognize: the name of a valet of Louis XIV or of an actor in Molière's company which came here in 1669 and 1670.

Yet the merest scrutiny suggests that a great number of the old dates are false. I don't think we should be saddened by the fact. The silly visitor who, cutting his name with the tip of his penknife, adds a date which rejuvenates it by three hundred years, becomes the unconscious auxiliary of an historical "demythification."

It is not enough, indeed, that Chambord, a residence often scorned by the sovereigns who succeeded each other since the first years of the Renaissance (Henry IV never set foot in it, Louis XIII appeared there only once, Louis XIV stopped visiting it thirty years before the end of his reign, Louis XV and Louis XVI had never heard of it), should exist outside the official legend and outside History. It is also good that the past, for us a source of emotion once it appears in any more or less intimate form, should be the object of imitations, of counterfeits, and can thus be held in suspicion. We can acquire esthetic objectivity and achieve what is infinitely more important, access to the domain of the secret, only by escaping the fascination of the old, the nostalgia of bygone days.

I know that this nostalgia, this emotion results from an initial astonishment —it is fundamental to our race, which alone has had the evil genius of introducing into life the agonizing awareness of time. I know that it is in our destiny to seek the repetition of this astonishment from which, once, we have derived an enlivening pleasure. The notion of time remains man's surest damnation. How, without palpable proofs, could he really feel that he existed, even three centuries ago?

An old date, cut into the stone, is enough to plunge him into a comforting stupor. This date exorcises the night, the nothingness. But a stone and a date are still not enough: around them subsists a void more frightening than our death: the void of

East front of the château.
On the right, southeast tower of the keep.
In the center, wing of François I

our absence. Other proofs must be furnished, always more proofs! We shall never be done convincing ourselves that we are not the first to have to die.

So this infinite multitude of the dead must rise, each of whom holds a carved stone, a painted canvas, a piece of writing, a rusty helmet, a chest or a humble object, the first thing at hand, it doesn't matter : a piece of pottery, a bit of frayed cloth. And henceforth we are a prey to a frenzy rather like that of the lost dog given a piece of clothing that belonged to its master. Lost in time, with others lost like ourselves, we scent a human odor dominating that of a funereal corruption, and we rediscover the paths of a living eternity. Yet how deny that we are blinded by this constant concern for human justifications, for references in the past, this feverish spotting of fording stones in the waters of oblivion, of absence? Outside of constructed History, of History materially present, there is so much to see, so much to live! We shall soon be imprisoned, bound fast as by a gigantic moraine or as at the center of a beaver dam!

Too many stones, too many vestiges. The humanism of the past is already giving way to a fetishism of the past. Where is the nakedness of man, of my brother forever present, unchanged— whom I find again in the British Museum, for instance, after having passed the Rosetta stone "almost without seeing it"— in this scarcely withered corpse five thousand years old and lying curled up like a hound on a few stones, a little pile of sand? To ask the question is, of course, to answer it. This man died, barely a moment ago, or is asleep, or, better still, I dream myself sleeping through him. The same is true of Chambord. By what it brings me, Chambord is five thousand years old, and has no age, no years at all.

Up to now I have had to follow, more or less, with this château, a chronology that favored, that flattered my habitual feelings which include, obviously, not a little nostalgia. This was inevitable, it was in the order of things: one must never forbid oneself feelings. There is the music, so terribly convincing and "livable," and then the truth, I mean: the truth beyond.

In trying to rediscover the truth, I have proceeded in the manner of a painter. When he comes to the point of no longer seeing clearly what he is doing, the painter sometimes turns his back on his picture and walks as far away from it as the size of his studio permits. Thus, on several occasions, after having wandered through the château for a long time, I left it, either because other obligations made is necessary or because I felt the need to do so.

In this latter case, I preferred to take a path which, on the other side of the Cosson, vanished into the trees, parallel to the château whose northern front, through the branches stripped by winter, took a certain time to vanish from sight. This little forest path was curiously named *la route de l'Oubli*, the road of oblivion, a name I was quick to make into a kind of recipe. As long as it was still visible, I was careful not to look at the château. I thought only of the trees, which in winter doesn't take one very far. I thought of the stones of the path, the coming rain. . . .

In the same way, the painter, having turned his back on the subject that is too much for him and having moved away, finds himself with his nose against the wall and forces himself to stare at it a long time, to let himself be invaded by the greatest mental inertia (but make no mistake, it is often, too, the deceptive silence of despair). For me, however, there was no question of despair: I was not building Chambord, merely inhabiting it and trying to understand it. To understand it? What an idea!

I was going to take the *route de l'Oubli* back, to face, once again, that bright façade with, above, the accumulation of chimneys, roofs, and campaniles that suggests those lofty cities one sees above the horizon, in mirages. And it sometimes happens, I would think of that bright façade, that famous upper city—and have absolutely no desire to face them again. It would have been so easy for me to continue on my way! Behind me, there was doubtless nothing to understand. Yet I turned around and walked back: there was, perhaps, nothing to understand, but "I was expected." By whom? No one nameable or imaginable, of course: I am not going to fall into romantic dramatization and evoke the ghosts of the past. I merely want to speak, here, about that patient expectation of the work of art which, deep in the galleries

of a museum, erodes the shadow or which, in this French countryside, hastens a little the dawn, delays a little the evening. An expectation that is, also, our own.

Then I accepted Chambord again—completely. Not in an impulse of sentimentality, as it might seem, but with application and the greatest possible lucidity. I was careful not to yield to the fascination of History and, as I approached the château, not to excite myself by the thought that this was how it looked, four centuries ago, to the traveler. It did not look like this. The woods came closer, apparently; the highway wasn't here; the Cosson had been diverted; moats filled with water surrounded the structure until the eighteenth century; the lantern wasn't the same, though the copy made in 1891 was a faithful one; as for the stained glass that embellishes it . . . In short, with regard to the reflection of History, a great—and inevitable— share of lies.

What I would have to see, then, henceforth, was Chambord in its novelty, its perpetual novelty. What I would have to discover was this strange presence literally coming out of ambush at the corner of the woods where the *route de l'Oubli* runs, this unwonted construction that appeared here only a moment before, offering itself impassively to all the tricks of perspective, slowly releasing, as I circled it, a tower, a campanile, then warily withdrawing it in order to thrust another one out onto the stage. What I would have to discover was this "event," as if the whole, in its moving perfection, had fallen from the sky, as attested by its amber-tinged whitness almost as embarrassing as the light that surrounds celestial structures in edifying paintings.

Once the shadows retained by the upper portion had vanished, I found myself in the presence of an ideal reality, a miraculous accident plunging the surrounding countryside into the silence of a slow fascination. Doubtless, as I approached, I would glimpse, in the structure, certain shrill or somber parts, as they withdrew into History and secrecy. Doubtless I would again be overwhelmed and everywhere surrounded by these countless shapes of stone which, encompassing me within an ever-closer labyrinth, would band my thought to their volutes, to the designs of their ornaments, submit me to the silence of the mysterious carved figures and, holding me thus a prisoner in a dream, soon keep me from knowing what was Chambord, what myself.

The reader, through these pages, will have felt the spell to which, consenting for the most part, I have been subject, a spell that has made me find again, however often I stumble, the path to that city—radiant and dark, wise and wild, silent and haunted—which we bear within ourselves.

Technical and historical notes

compiled by
Paul Robert-Houdin,
curator of the Château
of Chambord

Château of Chambord.
Nineteenth-century lithograph

The Château of Chambord
from the Place d'Armes
Nineteenth-century lithograph

Chambord, in the sixteenth century, was called Chambour (by Ronsard), Chambourg (by Rabelais, in Gargantua, and by Clément Marot who, in a letter, writes, "They say that at Chambourg it is fair"). According to the etymologists, the name comes from a modification of the old word "cambourg," from "camb," a curve, since the Cosson, a tributary of the Beuvron, may, at one time have curved at the spot where the château was later to be built. It is situated in the commune of Bracieux, on the western borders of Sologne, 3 ½ miles from the Loire, 10 from Blois, and 103 from Paris, at the point where the forests of Bussy and Boulogne meet. Its 33,606-acre park is today the property of the State, and constitutes a sort of reserve so thickly populated with game that it becomes necessary every year to destroy a large number of wild boars. The visitor will also encounter a great many deer which, since they are no longer hunted, often allow him to come quite close. There exists no document that sheds any light on the reasons that led François I to choose Chambord as the site for a château of such magnitude: Abundance of game (since hunting was the chief pastime of the aristocracy at this period)? The king's fondness for this district where, as a young man, he had often lived (at Romorantin, at Blois, at Amboise)? Sentimental memories? It is true that a building, of whose appearance no record survives, already existed on this site. In the tenth century, it belonged to Thibault le Tricheur, Comte de Blois, and passed

to his descendants. In 1183, 1189, and 1190, Thibault le Bon signed three charters there. During the Hundred Years' War, Chambord was equipped for defense, and in July, 1356, the Comte de Blois installed a small garrison there. In 1411 Chambord served as a prison (or gehyne, as the texts of the period say) for the Sire de Crouy, convicted of complicity in the assassination of the Duc d'Orléans. Finally, we learn from the archives that during the fifteenth century the château was occupied by a capitaine de roi. In all likelihood François I then had it razed, but we may assume that if no trace of it remains, it is because the new château stands on exactly the same spot. Parts of the old masonry and foundations may have been utilized for the new building, which would explain the element of inconsistency which we find in the general conception of the new Chambord. The château was begun in about 1519. But what architect drew up the plan? There exist two opposing theories: the first attributes the château to an Italian, the second to the master masons of Blois. The partisans of the first theory have, however, renounced the claim that the author of the original plans was Leonardo da Vinci. The great Italian master died, in fact, in the same year that digging began on the foundations; and some historians suspect that the king even waited for him to die before commiting this "infidelity." Who the true architect was we have yet to learn. Up till the end of the nineteenth century, the names

of Vignola (Giacomo Barozzi, author of the Treatise on the Five Orders of Architecture) and Primaticcio were frequently mentioned. Since the first was born in 1507 and the second in 1504, however, and participation on their part could only have occurred very late in the day. An order was discovered in 1880, dated 1532, granting 900 livres to the architect Domenico Barnabei da Cortona, called "le Boccador," the architect of the old Hôtel de Ville in Paris, "as recompense for several pieces of work done during the last fifteen years by order and command of the King, projects drawn up and wooden models, both for constructions in the city and for the châteaux of Ardres, Tournay, Chambour . . . ." In the following century, the architect and art historian André Félibien drew up a plan from a wooden model of Chambord that he attributed to "le Boccador." However, this plan shows many notable differences from the château as we know it. The great square keep with its four flanking towers at the corners is the only element depicted exactly as we see it today. The champions of the theory that the building is essentially the work of the master masons of Blois took this plan as an argument in their favor, and put forward several names, notably that of Jacques Sourdeau. Documents in the archives prove that he took part in the work between 1519 and 1521. From 1522 to 1538, another master mason, Pierre Trinqueau, was at Chambord, where he directed, chiefly, the construction of the keep. Then came Jacques Coqueau,

Left : Finial of the great staircase. Engraving by Le Rouge. Eighteenth century

Right : Royal salamander decorating the vault of the staircase leading to the bedroom of François I. Etching by Goujean. Nineteenth century.

Engraving by Androuet Du Cerceau.
Sixteenth century

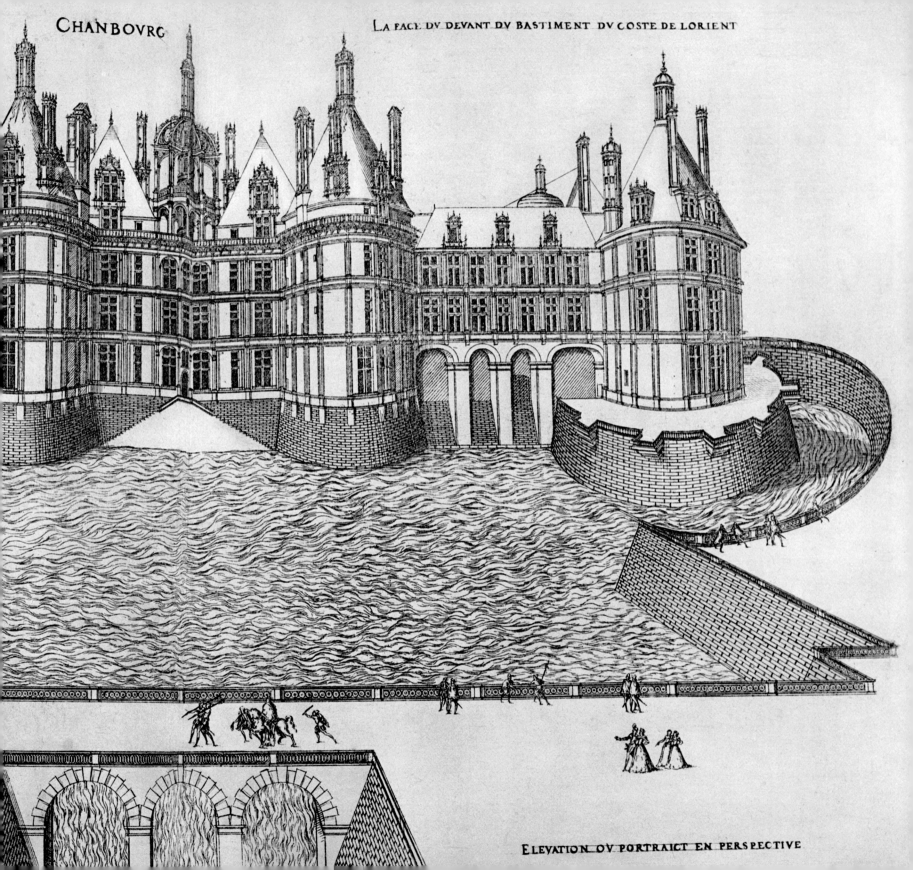

CHANBOVRG

LA FACE DV DEVANT DV BASTIMENT DV COSTE DE LORIENT

ELEVATION OV PORTRAICT EN PERSPECTIVE

D. LANCELOT

who built the two wings, though he left the west one unfinished. Nevertheless, in 1539, François I was able to entertain Charles V at Chambord and hear him declare that this château was in his eyes "a summary of what may be achieved by human industry," which indicates that a great part of the work was already a reality. The keep had been finished in 1533, the roof terraces in 1537. Work was about to begin on the two wings, though the west wing was destined to remain only partly finished even under Henri II, and work was still going on there when Louis XIV came to the throne. In 1557, the Venetian Ambassador, Lippomano, wrote of Chambord: "More than half is still to be built, and I doubt that it will ever be possible to finish it." Though the details may always remain somewhat confused, the chronology of the château's construction may be established as follows:

1519 Letters patent authorizing the work, given at Blois, September 6. François de Pontbriand named as superintendent of works. The marshy nature of the soil makes work on the foundations difficult. Work interrupted from July, 1524, to September, 1526, first because of financial difficulties and also because of the captivity of the king, who hab been taken prisoner at Pavia (February 24, 1525). The king's return was followed by a period of great activity. For roughly the next twelve years, 1800 workmen were employed at Chambord.

1534 Mention is made of work being started on the preparation of the timbering.
1537 The towers and pavilion of the keep are built.
1538 The keep is almost finished.
1543 Construction of the staircase in the wing of François I.
1545 The apartments adjoining this staircase are nearly completed. Work is begun on the wall around the grounds (more than 18 miles long).
1547 Death of François I. Henri II orders work to continue on the west wing and on the chapel tower.
1550 A certain Louisières, known as "Vendôme," a master carpenter living in Blois, executes plans and drawings for the timbering of the chapel roof.
1556 Claude de Bombelles is ordered to continue and bring to completion the buildings and the enclosing wall of the grounds.
1559 Death of Henri II. From this point onward, all work on the château seems to have been abandoned.

Apart from revealing, to a certain degree, how the foundations of the original medieval building were used in the construction of the present château, a scrutiny of the plan of Chambord as it stands emphasizes the typically French character of the topographical arrangement of the whole building. "During the first part of the sixteenth century, the general topographical arrangement created in the Middle Ages for royal and feudal fortresses was conserved: a vast quadrilateral with pavilions

The guardroom.
Nineteenth-century etching

or towers at the corners." (M. Vachon,
La Renaissance française. L'Architecture
nationale, *Paris, 1910). This character*
inherited from the feudal castle
and fortress was also to be found
in the château of Bonnivet, begun
in 1512 for Gouffier, Grand Amiral
de France, and in the château
of Chantilly, begun in 1522 (the first
of these was destroyed in 1522,
the second almost completely rebuilt).
Vincennes (which of course predates
Chambord by almost two hundred years),
and Bury, in the valley of the Cisse,
also spring from the same conception.
Lastly, Talcy, in Beauce, which dates
from the beginning of the
sixteenth century, with its central keep,
its corner turrets, its wings built out
from the keep, and its enclosed
court yard, constitutes one of the
purest examples of the French style
of the period. The round feudal
towers disappear for the
first time with the construction of
Saint-Maur, in 1540, under
the influence of Philibert de l'Orme,
who, in one of his books
twenty-five years later, was to
represent the "bad architect" as still
building round, crenelated towers.
In fact, round towers were still built,
in some provinces, up till the end of the
eighteenth century, because the great
lords remained attached to them
as token of their feudal power.
As far as Chambord is concerned,
its medieval aspect was accentuated
by the existence of moats of running
water directly under the walls.
The course of the Cosson was slightly
diverted to achieve this effect. Later,

through lack of maintenance, the water
became stagnant; and in the
eighteenth century King Stanislas of
Poland, who was living there at
the time, had the moats filled in.
If the general conception of the château
calls to mind the French style
of the early sixteenth century and
shows no trace of the Italian spirit
of that period, the interior and
exterior ornamentation of the building,
on the other hand, may be taken as
evidence of the influence or even the
intervention of artists from Italy. In the
first half of the sixteenth century,
château roofs suddenly began to reach
up much higher than the roofs of
the Middle Ages; they began to
bristle with colossal chimneys, gables,
bell towers, etc. This was a break
with French tradition. The same is true
of the ornamentation of the interior.
"For the more or less richly painted
ceiling beams of the fifteenth century,
the Renaissance substitutes the wood
or stone compartmented ceiling
with pendent bosses at the points
of intersection . . . ." (H. Clouszot,
Notes sur "Gargantua"). *And it was*
Primaticcio, arriving in France in about
1531, who first introduced coffered
plasterwork ceilings at Fontainebleau.
Thus a certain "Italianism" in the
roofs and decorative elements of
Chambord cannot be denied. There
remains the double spiral staircase
constituting the center of the keep.
This is still, in its general conception,
a spiral staircase of the Middle Ages.
Generally speaking, the Renaissance
was content to develop this concept
into an open staircase with a

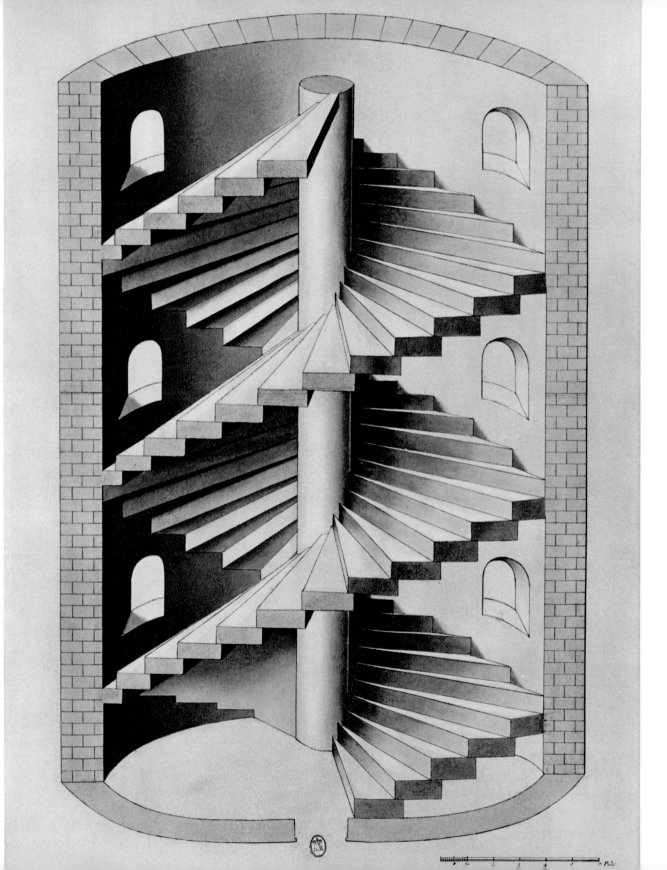

Cross section
of the staircase.
Seventeenth-century
drawing.

Watercolor by Charlotte El Burgess.
Nineteenth century

*balustrade and, to use the term
of the period, a "broken screw" in
other words, a spiral staircase into
which landings or "rests" have been
introduced. The double spiral staircase
at Chambord seems to be a copy
of the one in the Church of the Bernadines
(the cornerstone of which was laid
in May 1338). This "formed
two stairways turning the one on the
other, having the heads of their treads
inserted in the same newel, in such
wise that two people could go up and
come down without seeing each other.
This double staircase was ten feet
in diameter . . . ."* (Tableau historique
et pittoresque de Paris, *1811). The
diameter of the staircase at Chambord
is at least twice as great, and,
to return to the opposing "French"
and "Italian" theories of the château's*

*origin, it should be noted that in
Félibien's drawing after "le Boccador's"
model there figures a straight Italian
staircase. Nevertheless there is a final
point in favor of the defenders of
the "Italian" theory—the slate
lozenges and circles which we find
decorating the outside of the château
in such profusion are, without any possible
doubt, an imitation of the black marble
ornamentation so typical of Italian
architecture at that time. At Chambord
there was no marble to be had. In
the surrounding district, however, there
was stone in abundance. The quarries
of Vineuil, Saint-Gervais, and
Pont-Levoy provided the hard stone
for the construction of the château;
the softer stone came from the valleys
of the Cher and the Indre, from Bourré,
Lyé, Apremont, Marnays, and Cheillé.*

The soft stone from Bourré was used a great deal because it is so splendidly suited to sculpture. It is to be regretted that it was not used for the various restorations. The slate naturally came from Angers. The wood was provided by the surrounding forest, which includes many different species. The main woods used were chestnut, which worms do not attack, and oak.

The Restorations

1666 Louis XIV asks Jean de la Saussaye, and later Mansard, to draw up a plan for the restoration of the château. It is said that the king intended to build two wings on the Place d'Armes in front of the present south front, to be used as stables and outhouses. Thus there would have been an outer court enclosed by a grille. This first part of the project went no further than the most timid attempts at execution. The second part, on the other hand, was fully realized. It consisted of covering the buildings forming the south side of the courtyard, the two corner towers, and the ends of the François I and Henri II wings with "Mansard" roofs. Apart from this, Mansard restored several other parts of the château, in particular three large rooms on the second floor of the keep on the north side.
1725 to 1733 Stanislas Leczinski has the moats filled in, changes the course of the Cosson, and plans the gardens.
1733 to 1948 No work on the château. However, in accordance with an order

by the Council of State, 114 new rides are cut through the grounds in order to facilitate the hunt.
1748 The Maréchal de Saxe, now living in the château, has barracks built on the spot Mansard had chosen for the same purpose. They are destined to be destroyed by fire in 1794.
1828 The Duchesse de Berry lays the cornestone of the restoration of Chambord, on the "Oratoire" terrace. Political events subsequently prevent the undertaking of this work.
Between 1830 and 1848, most of the mansard roofs put in by Mansard built over the outbuildings are removed.
1881 The Bourbon princes entrust the work of restoring the château to the architect Deboise. The floors of the great guardrooms and the roof timbers are reconstructed and the slate covering replaced. Several architectural details destroyed by time are reconstructed.
1892 The lantern, in imminent danger of collapse, is taken down stone by stone. A new lantern, exactly copied from the old, is then put up in its place. Minor restorations continue until 1914.
1925 Since the château is still in receivership, the State undertakes the restoration of the balustrades on the roof terraces of the keep and the staircases of François I and Henri II. The roofs are reslated, the remainder of Mansard's "improvements" demolished, and terraces built over the outbuildings.

At the present time, considerable funds have been voted for the further restoration of Chambord, and work of various kinds is now in progress.

Plan of the grounds of Chambord. Engraving by N. Desmadryl. Nineteenth century

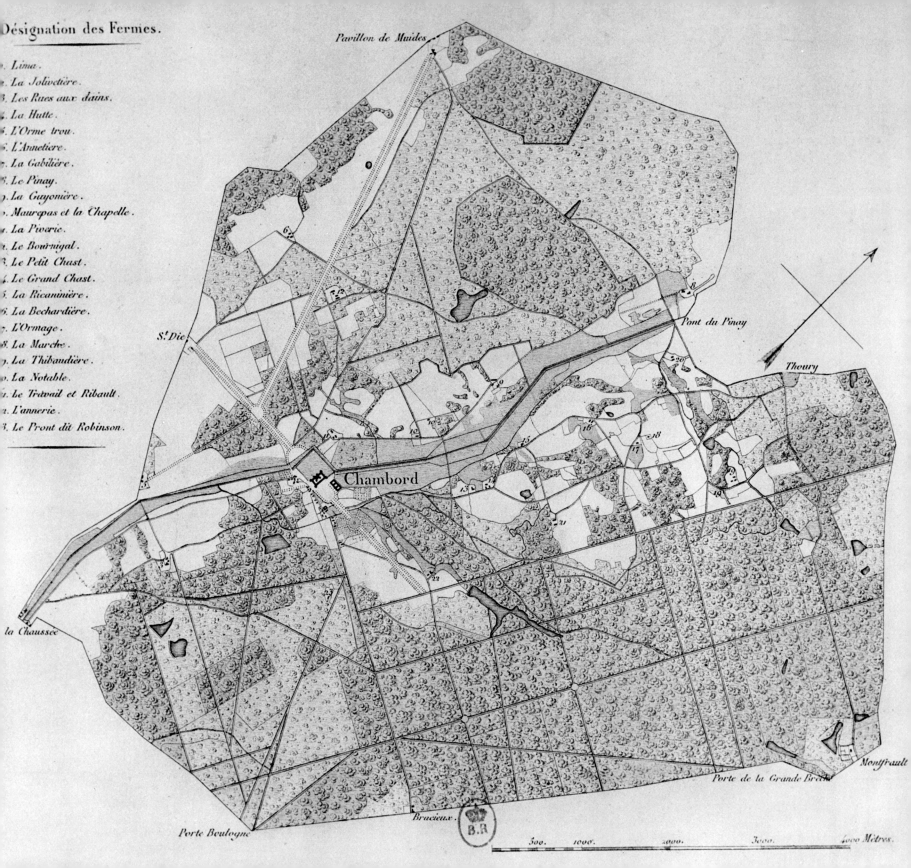

Désignation des Fermes.

1. Lima.
2. La Jolivetière.
3. Les Rues aux dains.
4. La Hutte.
5. L'Orme trou.
6. L'Annetière.
7. La Gabilière.
8. Le Pinay.
9. La Guyonière.
10. Maurepas et la Chapelle.
11. La Piverie.
12. Le Bournigal.
13. Le Petit Chast.
14. Le Grand Chast.
15. La Ricaninière.
16. La Bechardière.
17. L'Ormage.
18. La Marche.
19. La Thibaudière.
20. La Notable.
21. Le Tratvail et Ribault.
22. L'annerie.
23. Le Pront dit Robinson.

Pavillon de Muides.

S.t Die.

Pont du Pinay.

Thoury.

Chambord

la Chaussée.

Montfrault

Porte de la Grande Brèche

Porte Boulogne   Bracieux.   B.R.

500.   1000.   2000.   3000.   4000 Mètres.

What was happening in the world from 1519 to 1550

1519 Magellan sailing around the world
Death of Leonardo da Vinci at Amboise
Charles V elected Emperor
Parley on the Field of the Cloth of Gold

1520 Spaniards expelled from Mexico
Death of Raphael
Luther excommunicated

1521 Death of Magellan in the Philippines
Beginning of the war between
François I and Charles V
Suliman the Magnificent takes Belgrade
Cortez subjugates Mexico

1522 First public loan in France
Luther's Bible

1523 Henry VIII devalues British currency
Treason of the Duc de Bourbon,
last of the great feudal barons in France

1524 Death of Bayard (and loss
of the State of Milan for the French)
October: François I reconquers Milan

1525 Pavia. François I loses Milan
for good and is taken prisoner
Battle of Mohács. Hungary becomes
an Ottoman protectorate
Naples and Rome lose nine-tenths
of their populations from the plague

1526 The banker Hochstetter,
quicksilver king, controls the minting
of coin throughout Europe
Treaty of Madrid

1527 The troops of Charles V sack Rome
Sweden, under Gustavus Vasa,
converts to Lutheranism

1528 Famine in Tuscany

1529 Charbot sails up the Uruguay
and the Paraná
The Turks encamp before Vienna
Peace of Cambrai

1530 Augsburg Confession, creed
of Lutheranism
Collège de France founded in Paris

1531 On August 24 Pedro de Mendoza,
with 2,000 men and 11 ships, founds
Buenos Aires
Beginning of the Wars of Religion
in Germany

1532 Pizarro and Almagro land in Peru
Calvin expelled from France
Rabelais publishes "Pantagruel"

1533 Birth of Montaigne
Henry VIII repudiates Catherine of
Aragon and marries Anne Boleyn

1534 Jacques Cartier in Canada

1536 The "Capitulations" between
François I and Suliman seal the
Franco-Turkish alliance and allot to
France the rôle of protector of the
Christians in the Ottoman Empire
Exploration of Texas by Cabeza de Vaca
Calvin publishes "l'Institution chrétienne"
Death of Erasmus
Henry VIII executes Anne Boleyn
and marries Jane Seymour

1538 Henry VIII excommunicated

1539 Meeting of François I and
Charles V at Chambord

1540 Henry VIII marries Anne of Clèves
Henry VIII repudiates Anne of Clèves
Henry VIII marries Catherine Howard

Orellana descends the Amazon
from Peru to the sea

1541 Ferdinand, brother of Charles V,
defeated at Buda.
Charles V defeated at Algiers
Roberval founds the colony of Canada
Valdivia founds Santiago in Chile

1542 The Portuguese establish
a settlement in Canton
The German princes convert
to Protestantism
Henry VIII executes Catherine Howard
Alliance between Henry VIII
and Charles V

1543 Turkish fleet bombards Nice
Henry VIII marries Catherine Parr
"The Revolutions of the Celestial
Spheres" by Copernicus. His death
Battle of Cerisoles

1544 The Turks in Toulon,
Charles V in Meaux,
the English in Boulogne, Treaty of Crépy

1545 Council of Trent
Massacre of the Vaudois in France

1546 Rabelais publishes his "Tiers livre"
Pierre Lescot begins the Louvre
Death of Luther

1547 Death of Henry VIII
Death of François I

1548 Du Bellay: "Défense et illustration
de la langue française"

1550 Ronsard: "Odes"
The silk industry of Lyon employs
12,000 workers

JACQUES I DU CERCEAU, *architect and engraver (1510-1585): "The whole edifice is admirable to the eye and of superb and wonderful aspect."*

JÉROME LIPPOMANO, *Venetian ambassador to the court of Henri II: "I have seen, in my life, many magnificent constructions, but never one richer or more beautiful than this... We left Chambord amazed, confounded..."*

NICOLAS-FRANÇOIS BLONDEL, *architect of the Porte Saint-Denis (1618-1686): "The staircase of this château, seen from the terrace, strikes one with such astonishment that it is all but impossible to conceive how anyone could have imagined such a picturesque design."*

ALFRED DE VIGNY: *"Suddenly one encounters a château that is royal, and yet less royal than it is magical. It seems as though some Genii of the East, compelled by the power of a wonderful lamp, lifted it from the ground during one of the Arabian nights and stole here with it from sunnier climes..."*

VIOLLET-LE-DUC: *"The parody of a feudal castle !"*

1499 Palais de Justice in Rouen
1501 Hospicio in Compostella
1503 Bramante designs the gardens of the Vatican
1506 The cornerstone of Saint Peter's is laid in Rome
1513 Chenonceaux

1514 Hampton Court
1518 St-Pierre in Caen
1519 Chambord
1520 Azay-le-Rideau
Wing of François I at Blois
1521 S. Giustina in Padua
1528 Fontainebleau

1532 St-Eustache in Paris
1534 Palazzo Farnese in Rome
Chancellerie of Bruges
1535 Castle of Hartenfels at Torgau
1539 Château of St-Germain-en-Laye
1546 The Louvre
1550 Palazzo Chiericati at Vicenza

FELIBIEN. *Mémoires pour servir à l'histoire des maisons royales et bastimens de France.* 1681 *(A. de Montaiglon. Paris, 1874)*

LE ROUGE. *Description de Chambord, with 13 plates, 1750*

L. DE LA SAUSSAYE. *Le château de Chambord, Blois, 1828*

J. T. MERLE. *Chambord. Paris, 1832 (V. Canel)*

DE SOURDEVAL. *Chambord. In Mémoires de la société archéologique de Touraine. Volume III. Tours, 1845, 1846, 1847*

DE LAVERGNE. *Ruines pittoresques historiques de France. Paris, 1859*

L. PALUSTRE. *Le château de Chambord. La France artistique et monumentale, Volume IV*

G. EYRIES AND P. PERRET. *Les châteaux historiques de la France. Paris, Poitiers, 1879*

L. JARRY. *Le château de Chambord, documents inédits sur la date de sa construction et le nom de ses premiers architectes. Orléans, 1888*

G. DREUX. *Chambord, le château et son histoire. Chambord, 1904*

F. BOURNON. *Blois, Chambord et les châteaux du Blésois. Paris, 1908*

H. GUERLIN. *Le château de Chambord. H. Laurens, Paris, 1912*

P. LESUEUR. *Dominique de Cortone, dit le Boccador. Paris, 1928*

Mᵐᵉ CURY-PERON. *Le maréchal de Saxe. à Chambord. Bulletin de la Société amicale du Loir-et-Cher, Paris, 1927*

J. CASTELNAU. *Le maréchal de Saxe*

V. NADAL AND J. A. GRENOUILLOT. *Chambord, son château et son histoire, Blois, 1946*

E. DE GANAY. *Le château de Chambord. Paris, 1949*

DR. F. LESUEUR. *Léonard de Vinci et Chambord, in Etudes d'art, nos. 8, 9 and 10. Paris-Algiers, 1953, 1954*

P. ROBERT-HOUDIN AND G. MONMARCHE. *La féerie nocturne des châteaux de la Loire. Hachette, Paris, 1954*

F. GEBELIN. *Les châteaux de la Loire. Alpina, 1957*

Numerous documents in the National Archives, the Archives of the department of Loir-et-Cher, the Bibliothèque Nationale, and the Archives of the government office for Historical Monuments.

DATE DUE